T0131714

Thunder 'n Lightning
Explain

What it's like to die...

By
Kevin Lee Weaver
Illustrator: Dennis Lynn

Order this book online at www.trafford.com
or email orders@trafford.com

Most Trafford titles are also available at major online book retailers.

Print information available on the last page.

ISBN: 978-1-4120-3704-4 (sc)

Because of the dynamic nature of the Internet, any web addresses or links contained in this book may have changed since publication and may no longer be valid. The views expressed in this work are solely those of the author and do not necessarily reflect the views of the publisher, and the publisher hereby disclaims any responsibility for them.

Our mission is to efficiently provide the world's finest, most comprehensive book publishing service, enabling every author to experience success. To find out how to publish your book, your way, and have it available worldwide, visit us online at www.trafford.com

Any people depicted in stock imagery provided by Getty Images are models, and such images are being used for illustrative purposes only.
Certain stock imagery © Getty Images.

Trafford rev. 10/02/2018

www.trafford.com

North America & international
toll-free: 1 888 232 4444 (USA & Canada)
fax: 812 355 4082

ARON'S STORY

Hi ! My name is Aron. I'm sixteen now and I have been fighting Cancer for over
four years. The cancer started after I was diagnosed with Epstein-Barr after my kidney transplant.
The cancer I have is called Hodgkin's Lymphoma.
 (Please read my definitions, they will explain all of these new and big words.)
Anyway, I am here to help you understand about cancer, death and dying, Heaven and eternal life.
I am dying, I am terminally ill. I will not get better without help from doctors and nurses,
and all of the people who work in the hospital.
I will not give up!
I always wanted to be a nurse so I could help people and kids. Because of my cancer, I may never
get to grow up and become a nurse. So, I want to help now.
My story is pretty complicated, so I'll try to keep it as simple as I can. I have gone
through radiation, chemotherapy, and a stem cell transplant. All of these treatments have not worked.
Right now I am going through chemo again and a donor bone marrow transplant.
I have a lot of people in my corner (please read my poem-The Big Fight).
They are all my trainers...they are my angels.
My mom and dad are helping me through this awful time. My grandma and grandpa are helping too.
There are a lot of great people helping me. I am very lucky... I hope this helps everyone who reads it. If I
could help you with one thing that I have learned, it would be this... NEVER GIVE UP... FIGHT!
I'm not giving up... I am going to Fight! Fight! Fight!

Aron died September 18, 2004

ARON'S DEFINITIONS

Cancer-   Bad warrior (abnormal) cells that attack good healthy cells.

Death-   An interruption in the process or rhythm of life... (a parenthesis).

Dying-   The process (road) leading to death.

Eternal-   A process that never stops...it goes around and around.

Hodgkin's Lymphoma-   Bad warrior (cancer) cells in the lymph nodes.

Lymph Node-   Small round structures in the body that make good warrior cells.

Natural-   A process of nature... not fake...not artificial...it just is...it just happens

Normal-   A rhythm or pattern.

New Home-   (Heaven) The place where your soul is free.

Soul-   Deep inside your body...it's not your skin, your eyeballs or your hair. It's your mind... your emotions...(your intellect).

Terminally Ill-   Someone who is very sick... they're dying.

THE BIG FIGHT

While working out in the gym
I hear a voice, "Hey,"
he shoved me, "You wanna fight?"

I'm scared
I'm frightened
but I think...
"I'll take the chance!"

I work out for a month
I sweat and work out.
My Trainers say "Fight! Fight!"
I will give it my best.

ROUND 1
It's January...
I gave him my left, I gave him my right,
I think I knocked him out....
only to the count of nine.

ROUND 2
It's May...
I hear he wants to fight again-
I gave him my left, I gave him my right,
I fight and I fight
I think I knock him out...
again, only to the count of nine.

ROUND 3
It's December...
I hear he wants to fight once again-
I'm sure I'll give it my best.
I'll try to knock him out!

ROUND 4
It's May again...
The fight is on-
There are more rounds than I thought,
But that's okay.
I am going to win

In the corner I hear my Angels.

It was a sad, sad soggy day.
    Christopher Aron had been diagnosed with cancer-
        he was terminally ill.

The four cousin clouds gathered together and sagged.
    They hoped and prayed that little Christopher Aron
        would soon get well.

Cousin Boo-kee Boo was bluest of all.
But they all felt as helpless as four blue clouds could be
"What can we do to help little Christopher Aron?"
Boo-kee Boo cried. "Oh... I wish it was me!"

Zinging Zara bravely
tried to zing her zaniest zong.

But Zinging Zara was so sad
the zing in her zong was gone.

Little Princess Prislynn
  and her brother Rubby Rydan

they held each other very close...
and both started cryin'.

Sadly, Boo-kee Boo looked at each o
with a question in his eye.

As tears started down his cheeks,
he sobbed, "What is it like to die?"

Suddenly Thunder and Lightning rumbled and flashed.
They agreed, in symphonic reply,

"Simply simplify the simple explanation.
Now let's show them what it's like to die."

Gently Lightning lifted Little Princess Prislynn
the edge of his bolt.

He directed his attention to the other three clouds,
and to Boo-kee Boo he spoke.

Tenderly he warned, "Boo-kee Boo,
listen carefully to me...
never wish to take another one's place."

"I know right now you don't understand,
but death and dying
are very natural to the human race."

Softly, Thunder rolled, reinforcing his best friend's advice,

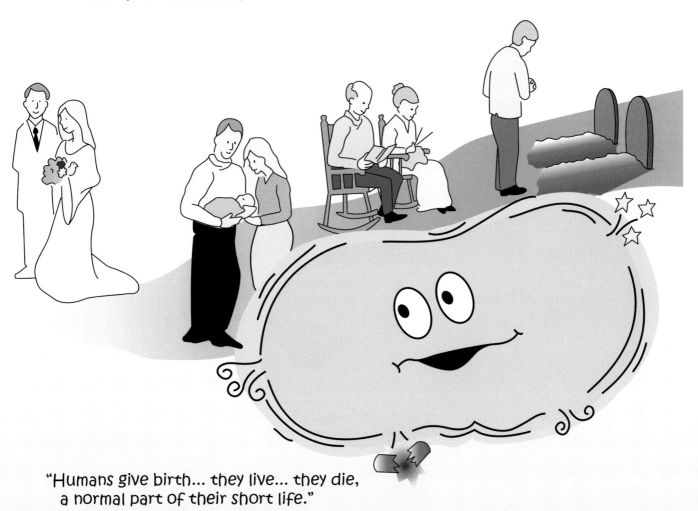

"Humans give birth... they live... they die, a normal part of their short life."

"It's like this," said Thunder as he picked up Rubby Rydan.
"You're a storm cloud in training... won't you agree?"
Rubby Rydan wiggled in Thunder's firm grasp,
"Yes Sir!" came the reply, "A storm in training... that's me!"

With that, Thunder began to squeeze Rubby Rydan-
    Thunder wringed and wranged the squeeze.
    Right before their eyes their friend turned into droplets...
        Zinging Zara cried, "Ru—bby!"

Then droplets formed a mist, gently falling to the ground.
And the cousin clouds were sad.
"Rubby Rydan was my best friend," Boo-kee Boo sniffed.
"Now he's gone... he's dead... I'm mad!"

Suddenly the sun began shining intensely...
Its warmth evaporating the mist.
The mist, which became a vapor, began to rise...
"Wow!" Boo-kee Boo exclaimed, "Look at this!"

Then to their stunned amazement
in wide-eyed wonder and awe-
a freshly changed and newly formed
Rubby is what they saw.

"Hey guys," Rubby funneled up,
  "you should have seen the things I saw."
  I was traveling fast. It was great..."
  Now Rubby was in awe.

"I saw molecules and atoms... protons-neutrons,
  and the inside of a rainbow.
  I had a glimpse of what dying is most like,"
  Rubby funneled down, "and now I know."

Zinging Zara and Little Princess Prislynn
opened their eyes very wide.
"Yippee!" Boo-kee Boo jumped for joy,
"Christopher Aron isn't gonna die!"

Quickly, Thunder interrupted,
"Hold on to your fluff for just a minute, little guys.
Listen very carefully to what we are saying.
Little Christopher Aron is going to die.
But the energy that is really him...
his soul... is going to a new home and will just be changing."

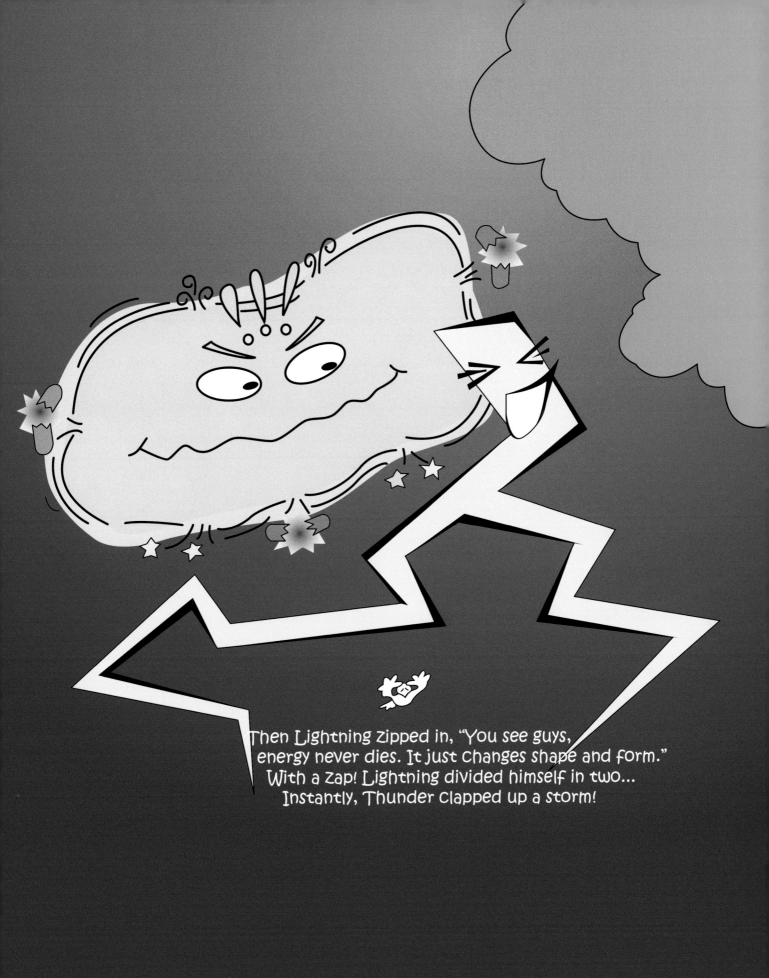

Then Lightning zipped in, "You see guys,
energy never dies. It just changes shape and form."
With a Zap! Lightning divided himself in two...
Instantly, Thunder clapped up a storm!

"Oh! I get it," zang Zinging Zara.
"Now it makes sense to me.
Eternal, like us clouds, is what
Little Christopher Aron will be!"

Boo-kee Boo chimed in,
"Oh yeah! I can see that too.
But before he dies
isn't there something we can do?"

"There is one thing we elements can do," Thunder thoughtfully added.
"We can ask of Father Time that quality and comfort be granted."
With a flick, Lightning complimented his friend's words of wisdom,
"Quality and comfort are the things Father Time can give him."

"Now here's where everything gets very tricky,"
Thunder rumbled and rolled and roared.
"Father Time can't do it all on his own.
With the help of humans and hospice...
together, they can guarantee
Christopher Aron a safe trip to his new home."

It was no longer a sad soggy day.
  And, as expected, Little Christopher Aron soon died.
  Boo-kee Boo reminded the others, "It's okay!
  He lives in our memory." Then Boo-kee Boo sighed.

Printed in the United States
By Bookmasters